I Want Peace with God

I WANT PEACE WITH GOD

Ephesians 1

18 I pray that the eyes of your heart may be enlightened in order that you may know the hope to which he has called you, the riches of his glorious inheritance in his people, 19 and his incomparably great power for us who believe.

Content

Acknowledgements

I would like to thank the following people who worked with me on this project and without whose labor this book would not exist.

- To John Hendee, whose study "A Peace Treaty with God" influenced much of my evangelism methodology and whose ideas greatly influenced the ideas contained in this study.

- To my wife, Jacqueline Galo-Canarsky, for her countless ideas and detailed editing.

- To Brayner Ruíz, for his untiring and excellent work with the graphic design and formatting of this book.

- To Jason and Cindy Nabb and Raquel Figueroa-Colon for their careful editing and excellent suggestions.

- To Marc Joyce for his great illustration of the separation between man and God, and the cross which gives us a path to God.

.

- To Karen O'Neal for the initial idea of the cover image.

- To Rachel Dermody for making a brilliant cover for the second version.

It is an enormous privilege for me to be able to work in the kingdom of our Lord with you!

- Philip Canarsky

Introduction

In life, there are many things that are important. We live lives that are completely occupied with important matters. We have family, work, bills to pay, debts, friendships and commitments. Have you ever thought about what is the most important thing in life?

I have thought a good deal about that question. What I have come to believe is that the most important thing in life is to know God. More important than anything else is knowing who God is and how to have peace with God.

In our world, there are a great variety of religions, churches and beliefs. Because of this, when we think about God, there is frequently a good deal of confusion around the question "How can I have peace with God?" It seems as if everyone has a different answer to that question.

In the book that we call the Bible, we find words that were inspired by God.[1] Which is why, in the Bible we can discover the message that God has for us. God reveals that every single person can come to know and have peace with Him.

(1) 2 Timothy 3:16

This book is a compilation of six studies through which we learn how we can know God and have peace with Him. I hope that these studies can serve as a guide to help you find peace with God.

How to Use
I Want Peace with God

We live in a world where there is a great deal of confusion about what it means to be a child of God, to have peace with God and to follow Christ. There are many religions, doctrines, traditions, beliefs, and spiritual practices. This is why it sometimes can be hard to explain the essence of what it means to have peace with God to our friends and family, and at times, even to ourselves.

I Want Peace with God is a study that explains how someone can come to have peace with his Creator.

This is a tool

This study is a tool to explain how to enter into peace with God. I Want Peace with God is a study that describes, briefly and concisely, what the Bible says about God and how to become his son or daughter.

We all have friends, relatives and loved ones that aren't at peace with God. At times in life, opportunities present themselves for us to explain to these people what the Bible says about how to have peace with God. Unfortunately, often we aren't prepared in these moments to be able to give a good explanation of our faith and how to enter into peace with God. So instead of speaking, we wait for a "better opportunity."

This study has been designed to be used in these moments, when one has the opportunity to talk with someone else about their faith and explain what it is they believe. It doesn't contain a detailed explanation of all the doctrines and traditions of different religions. Rather, it seeks to simply explain how to have peace with God.

Who is this study for?

I Want Peace with God was written for people that have already made their decision to follow Christ, as well as for those who are still investigating this idea.

For those who have already decided to follow Jesus, this study explains how a personal relationship with God functions. It describes what God's child receives from his Father and what his responsibilities are in this relationship.

For those who still haven't made the decision to enter into peace with God, this study clearly describes how to make that decision, and how someone can live the rest of his life at peace with God after surrendering to Him.

What is the goal of this study?

The goal of this study is that the person who hasn't entered into a relationship with God would come to the point of making the decision to completely surrender himself to God by making the decision to turn to God through repenting and being baptized, thereby entering into peace with God (Acts 2:38). It describes how important it is to make this decision, and why we should desire to cross the line of faith. It explains how to make the decision to become God's child. The last study provides a description of how to live life after making this decision.

How to study with someone

I would like to share with you a few suggestions of how you could use this study to help your friends and family members enter into peace with God. The following is a description of some of the most effective methods of using this study.

How to ask to study

In order to study with a friend or relative, one first must offer to study with him. This moment isn't the same for everyone, so one should offer the study when he feels led by the Spirit and perceives that the other person might be open to talking more about God.

- When I ask someone to study, I normally say something very direct, for example: "I wanted to ask you if you would like to study about what the Bible says about how to have peace with God?"

- Then, I mention what the studies are like by saying: "There are six studies, they normally take 25-35 minutes each. We could study one a week."

- If the person says "no," or if they make an excuse or offer a reason why they can't study, then the most important thing is to "leave the light on." In other words, let them know that this is fine, that it doesn't change anything in your friendship, and that they can study with you anytime they change their mind. You can say something like: "No problem, I just offered in case you were interested. If, later on, you'd like to study, just let me know and we'll study."

- However, if the person says "yes!" to your invitation to study, then it is very important to set up the appointment for the first study right then. It is too easy to say something like: "That is great! We will have to study sometime." By saying this, you aren't setting up the first study, and it is much less likely that they will actually do it. Instead, when they accept the idea of studying, you should immediately make the first appointment. You could say: "That's great! Why don't we get together this week? Is there a specific day or time that would work best for you?" By doing this, you start the ball rolling.

How to use this book

Normally, it is a good idea to take sufficient copies of this book to the study so that everyone you are studying with can read from their own copy. If you are studying with several people, it also works to share a few books between everyone. What's more, it isn't even necessary to use physical copies of the book; digital copies can be downloaded free of charge from www.IWantPeaceWithGod.com and read from a telephone or tablet.

After each study, it is best to take the books with you when you leave. The reason for this is so that you can all read the next study together, instead of everyone reading it beforehand.

At the end of each study, it is a very good idea to leave a copy of the summary handout (see the Appendix) for the study you just read, so that the person you are studying with can review it during the week.

The methodology

There are various things to remember when you are actually studying with someone.

First, it is important to go directly to the study. In other words, do not arrive, talk and let a long time go by before studying. It isn't bad to develop the friendship, but the study time flows much smoother if you get right into the study.

The method of giving the study that normally works best is to simply read it with the other person. When it is time to study, I normally say something along the lines of: "Why don't we study? Let's read the first study. If you have any questions while we read, just ask me. Would you like to take turns reading or would you prefer that I read everything?" Then, we start reading. I almost never stop the study until the end, unless the other person has a question.

When we reach the end of the study, I ask if they have any questions about what we read. Then, I give them the summary sheet of the study (see the Appendix), and tell them that it would be a good idea to review what we studied today during the next week, and that next time, we will start the study with any questions they might have.

The most important thing at the end of the study is to setup the appointment for the next study. I say something like: "Can we study again next week? Would the same day and time work?" By doing this, I make sure that the study continues.

This study is very important!

Let me end by reminding you of the priority we should put on this study. More specifically, if we are studying with someone, then one of the most important things in our lives is making sure that we complete the study with that person.

This is why, when we have an appointment for a study, we should make meeting that appointment our highest priority. We should even be willing to sacrifice our own time, schedule, desires, and agenda in order to complete the study.

Spiritual warfare

When you go through this study with someone, you are entering into a spiritual battle. The reason for this is that you are teaching someone far from God how to have peace with God. It is quite probable that the person with whom you are studying will make a decision and you will see him or her be baptized. Our enemy strongly desires that this not take place. In order to stop it from happening, he will attack you. You will feel discouragement, you will be held up, other appointments and commitments will present themselves, etc. The enemy knows that if he can dissuade you from doing the study, then the person you would have studied with will likely not enter the kingdom of God and, at least for right now, will not have peace with God.

It is extremely necessary to pray before, during and after each study. It is so essential to never miss a study that you have scheduled. It is also important to do each study with the great expectation that God will use this study to help the person you are studying with enter into peace with Him.

Chapter 1

We Need Peace

There is a need or a hunger that we all have: deep inside, we all want to be at peace with God. Maybe we don't always say it in that way, but this is a desire that God has put inside of every person.

We don't need more religion

When we hear "peace with God," often the first thing that came to our mind is religion. When we think of God, we often think of churches and cathedrals, ministers and priests, rituals and services, assemblies and mass, but we all know from experience that these things don't satisfy the internal desire we have for peace with God.

The need we feel inside isn't the need to have more religion, go to more services, be more religious, dress differently, or talk in a strange way. The need that we have is much deeper than a mere need for more religion.

We all need peace with God

The need that we all have is for peace with God. I have observed this need in myself and in others. It is a common need that we all have felt at different moments of our lives. Have you ever felt far away from God? Have you ever known someone else who felt far away from God?

This is something we feel sometimes when we are alone, when the television is turned off and we start to think about our lives. We know there is something more, something bigger than ourselves. That is the Being we call God. Many times at these moments, we feel like everything isn't OK between us and God.

The Bible says that this is a need that God Himself has placed inside us:

Acts 17

26 From one man he made every nation of men, that they should inhabit the whole earth; and he determined the times set for them and the exact places where they should live. 27 God did this so that men would seek him and perhaps reach out for him and find him, though he is not far from each one of us. 28 'For in him we live and move and have our being.' As some of your own poets have said, 'We are his offspring.'

God has put the desire to be at peace with Him inside of us.

Evidence of this need

We see the evidence of this need that God has put inside of each of us by how we live. It is as if we have a space or an emptiness inside, and all through life we search to fill this space with something, anything, that will make us feel complete.

It is an emptiness that is only filled when we encounter peace with God, but until we achieve that, we try to fill the emptiness with a wide variety of activities, vices and relationships.

So, when some people become addicted to alcohol or drugs, they are merely seeking to fill the emptiness they have inside.

When others jump from one intimate relationship to another, they are simply trying to feel complete inside.

When others become addicted to buying things and shopping, they are trying to fill the emptiness inside.

When others dedicate their lives to accumulating money, possessions, and riches, they are searching to feel complete inside.

When others spend all their time immersed in entertainment, sports, video games and parties, they are trying to satisfy the hunger they have inside that says there is something more to life.

What we discover is that none of these things truly fill us and make us complete. We are only complete when we fill that emptiness inside with God, when we finally have peace with God. Only peace with God brings peace to our lives.

Searching for peace

So, if you and I have the need to be at peace with God, then we have to ask ourselves the question, why don't we have peace with God?

Big Idea #1: We need peace with God because we are separated from God

The reason that we don't have peace with God is because, as humans, we are far from God. The Bible talks repeatedly about the separation that exists between people and God.

Why do you think there is such a huge separation between us and God?

Sin separates

The reason we are separated from God is because we sin. Sin is disobeying God. God says that the reason we are separated from Him is because we disobey. Our sin, our disobedience, separates us from God.

One of the major themes of the Bible is that our sin separates us from God.

Romans 3

23 for all have sinned and fall short of the glory of God,

Isaiah 59

1 Surely the arm of the LORD is not too short to save, nor his ear too dull to hear. 2 But your iniquities have separated you from your God; your sins have hidden his face from you, so that he will not hear. 3 For your hands are stained with blood, your fingers with guilt. Your lips have spoken lies, and your tongue mutters wicked things.

Colossians 1

21 Once you were alienated from God and were enemies in your minds because of your evil behavior.

Ephesians 2

12 remember that at that time you were separate from Christ, excluded from citizenship in Israel and foreigners to the covenants of the promise, without hope and without God in the world.

Sin is disobeying God

The definition of the word "sin" is to disobey God. There are two different ways that we disobey God.

The first is to do the bad things that He has said we shouldn't do. For example, rob, lie, envy, explode in anger, fornicate, talk badly about others, and many other things.

We also disobey God when we don't do the good things that He asks us to do. Some examples are: loving others, forgiving people when they hurt us, helping people in need and seeking to be close to Him.

Everyone disobeys

During our entire lives, each one of us disobeys God. We all disobey God. It is part of who we are. It doesn't matter how much we try, we can't live without disobeying God.

Romans 3

10 As it is written: "There is no one righteous, not even one;

Our disobedience separates us from God, so every time we disobey God, we become further and further separated from Him.

Disobedience separates because it is rebellion

I understand if it surprises you that all sin — even "little" sins — can separate us from God. At first, it doesn't make sense that all of our sin separates us from God. In order to understand why our sins separate us from God, we have to start by looking at the purpose that God has for us.

Created to be in communion

To better understand why sin separates us from God, we have to return to the beginning of creation and look at the purpose that God had when He made the man and woman.

The creation story documents that God made people in his own image.

Genesis 1

26 Then God said, "Let us make man in our image, in our likeness, and let them rule over the fish of the sea and the birds of the air, over the livestock, over all the earth, and over all the creatures that move along the ground." 27 So

God created man in his own image, in the image of God he created him; male and female he created them.

Later, in Genesis 3, it appears that God had the habit of walking through the garden where Adam and Eve lived, and spending time with them.

God made us in his image because He desires that we live in communion with Him.

Disobeying God is rebelling against Him

God made us to be in communion with Himself, but when we disobey Him, we are rebelling against Him. Our disobedience is a way of saying to God: "I don't care what you think or want from me, I am going to do what I think is best." In this way, we rebel against our Creator every time we disobey Him.

Romans 1

21 For although they knew God, they neither glorified him as God nor gave thanks to him, but their thinking became futile and their foolish hearts were darkened. 22 Although they claimed to be wise, they became fools 23 and exchanged the glory of the immortal God for images made to look like mortal man and birds and animals and reptiles. 24 Therefore God gave them over in the sinful desires of their hearts to sexual impurity for the degrading of their bodies with one another. 25 They exchanged the truth of God for a lie, and worshiped and served created things rather than the Creator--who is forever praised. Amen.

The Grand Canyon

In Arizona, there is an enormous canyon called the Grand Canyon. Through the middle of the canyon flows the Colorado river. As you can imagine, in between the two sides of the canyon there is an enormous distance.

We are far from God

Because we have rebelled against God, we are separated from Him. Our relationship with God is as if we were on one side of the Grand Canyon and God was on the other side. What separates us from God is our sin, or disobedience.

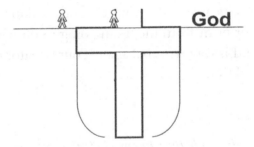

The distance between the two sides of the canyon reflects the emptiness that we feel inside. The need for peace with God that we feel is due to the fact that there is a great distance between God and us.

God punishes rebellion

Our sin doesn't just separate us from God. Eventually, it takes us to an eternity far from God. God has promised to severely punish our rebellion against Him.

Sin leads us to death

The hard truth is that God says in his word that when we disobey Him, we end up not only separated from Him in this life, but also separated from Him for eternity.

The Bible says that this is the death that our sin produces: spending eternity in torment and punishment separated from God.

Romans 6

23 For the wages of sin is death, but the gift of God is eternal life in Christ Jesus our Lord.

Revelations 21

8 But the cowardly, the unbelieving, the vile, the murderers, the sexually immoral, those who practice magic arts, the idolaters and all liars--their place will be in the fiery lake of burning sulfur. This is the second death."

Ephesians 2

3 All of us also lived among them at one time, gratifying the cravings of our sinful nature and following its desires and thoughts. Like the rest, we were by nature objects of wrath.

Romans 2

5 But because of your stubbornness and your unrepentant heart, you are storing up wrath against yourself for the day of God's wrath, when his righteous judgment will be revealed. 6 God "will give to each person according to what

*he has done." 7 To those who by persistence in doing good
seek glory, honor and immortality, he will give eternal life.
8 But for those who are self-seeking and who reject the
truth and follow evil, there will be wrath and anger.*

It is a harsh reality to consider that our sin takes us to
an eternity of torment far from God. However, this is
something we know is true, because God says it and also
because it is something we feel inside. This is why, when we
are separated from God, we feel so strongly this need to be
at peace with Him.

In Conclusion

- We all feel the need to be at peace with God.

- We all disobey God, we sin.

- Because of our sin, we are separated from
  God.

- Eventually, our sin leads us to an eternity
  without God.

Assignment

During this week, try to notice all the times you do things
you know you shouldn't:

- Every time you get mad

- Every time you speak poorly of someone else

- Every time you lie

- Every time you lose your patience

- Every time you become defensive

In these moments, reflect on this thought: "this is what separates me from a perfect God."

What we've seen so far:

- We need peace with God...because we are separated from God. (Chapter 1)

Chapter 2

The Bridge to Peace

In life, we all share the same problem: we disobey God and deserve his eternal punishment. This is what keeps us from being at peace with God. In order to enter into peace with God, we have to resolve this problem of our disobedience and the punishment that awaits us.

Someone has to pay the price of our punishment

Since we have disobeyed God, we are separated from Him and deserve his punishment. This is a reality that you and I can feel deep within our souls.

If we truly want to have peace with God, someone has to pay the price of our sin and literally take us to God.

Big Idea #2: Jesus is the bridge to God

Jesus, God's Son, came to this world as a man, lived a perfect life, and died a violent death on the cross. After dying, He was raised from the dead and now lives at God's side.

1 Corinthians 15

1 Now, brothers, I want to remind you of the gospel I preached to you, which you received and on which you have taken your stand.

3 For what I received I passed on to you as of first importance: that Christ died for our sins according to the Scriptures, 4 that he was buried, that he was raised on the third day according to the Scriptures,

By living a perfect life, He became the only person who has ever lived without sinning. He was the only perfect person who ever lived.

Because He was perfect, He didn't have to pay the price of his own sin, because He never sinned. So then when He died, He was able to pay with his death the price for the sin of every person on earth. He suffered and died for sin, not his own, but those of the whole world.

When He was raised to life, He broke the power of death. Now all of his followers have the true hope of being resurrected on the day when Jesus returns to this earth.

By paying the price for our sin, Jesus became our bridge to God.

Imagine a bridge over a canyon

If we are separated from God, as far from Him as two people on opposite sides of a huge canyon, Jesus is like the bridge that spans from one side of the canyon to the other. Through Him, we can go from where we are and be with God — at peace with God.

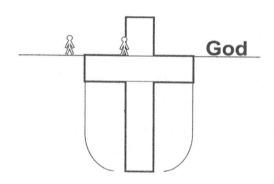

Jesus is the only way to God

Jesus said that He is the only way to God; that only through Him can you and I escape from the punishment of our sin, close the gap between God and us, and truly have peace with God.

John 14

6 Jesus answered, "I am the way and the truth and the life. No one comes to the Father except through me.

What Jesus is saying is that only He can take us to where we can have peace with God. There is no other religion, organization or lifestyle that can give us peace with God. Being good, going to church, or stopping bad habits cannot give us peace with God. Only Jesus can give us peace with God.

Jesus pays the price for our sin

By living a perfect, sinless life and dying an unjust death, Jesus paid the price for our sin.

1 Peter 2

24 He himself bore our sins in his body on the tree, so that we might die to sins and live for righteousness; by his wounds you have been healed.

When we sin, we deserve eternal death — which is God's just punishment, but Jesus paid the price of our sin by dying in our place.

Now, Jesus offers us forgiveness

Jesus offers us complete forgiveness for our sins. He forgives the sins we have committed in the past and the sins that we will commit in the future.

Romans 8

1 Therefore, there is now no condemnation for those who are in Christ Jesus,

1 John 2

2 He is the atoning sacrifice for our sins, and not only for ours but also for the sins of the whole world.

1 John 5

12 He who has the Son has life; he who does not have the Son of God does not have life.

Ephesians 2

4 But because of his great love for us, God, who is rich in mercy, 5 made us alive with Christ even when we were dead in transgressions—it is by grace you have been saved.

Even though it is difficult to accept the possibility that God would forgive us all of our sins, Jesus does offer complete forgiveness and pardon to every single person.

Jesus gives us peace with God

You and I can be at peace with God. In spite of the fact that we have disobeyed God in the past and will disobey God in the future, we can be at peace with God because Jesus offers forgiveness for all of our sins.

Romans 5

1 Therefore, since we have been justified through faith, we have peace with God through our Lord Jesus Christ,

This peace with God that Jesus offers can take us from where we are — far from God, to being forgiven and united with God the Father.

Jesus is the bridge to God

Jesus connects the two sides of the canyon of our sin that separates us from God; He takes us to God.

Colossians 1

13 For he has rescued us from the dominion of darkness and brought us into the kingdom of the Son he loves, 14 in whom we have redemption, the forgiveness of sins.

With his death, Jesus opened a way to God. That is why we can be at peace with God, in spite of having rebelled against our Creator.

We have to cross the bridge

Even though Jesus is the bridge between God and us, that doesn't mean that we are automatically at peace with God. In order to not be separated, we have to actually cross the bridge.

We have to make a decision

Any person can cross the bridge and be at peace with God. He only has to make a decision that he wants to cross over and become a child of God.

The Bible describes how we can make that decision.

Acts 2

38 Peter replied, "Repent and be baptized, every one of you, in the name of Jesus Christ for the forgiveness of your sins. And you will receive the gift of the Holy Spirit. 39 The promise is for you and your children and for all who are far off—for all whom the Lord our God will call."

In the next study, we will see what it means to make this decision to cross the bridge and enter into peace with God.

Assignment

During this week, every time you cross a bridge, think about Jesus. Think about how He is the bridge that can take you to God.

What we've seen so far:

- We need peace with God...because we are separated from God. (Chapter 1)
- Jesus is the bridge to God. (Chapter 2)

Chapter 3

Peace & Covenants

Who has peace with God? Everyone? Only a few? Just some? Some churches and religions almost make you feel that they think their members are saved. Other people use expressions like: "we are all God's children", as if we were all at peace with God.

If we all want to have peace with God, the most important question must be: Who actually has peace with God? In order to find the answer to this question, we have to see how God has related to people throughout time.

God has always offered peace to people through covenants (or agreements)

The Bible teaches that when God offers peace between himself and others, it is always through a covenant or an agreement. God offers the agreement, and the person who enters the agreement with God receives peace with God.

Big Idea #3: Only the person who has entered into an agreement with God has peace with God

We started with the question: Who has peace with God? The Bible teaches that only the person who has entered into a formal agreement with God has peace with God.

This is much more than just saying a prayer, going to church, reading the Bible, or stopping a sin. It is entering into an agreement with the living God of the Bible. Without being in a formal agreement with God, no one has peace with God. The history documented in the Bible shows that when someone enters into a formal covenant or agreement with God, he enters into peace with God.

What is the agreement with God like?

Like a contract

The agreements that God has offered throughout time to different men and women are somewhat like the contracts that we make when we do business.

In the following example, we can see how a covenant, whether it is a legal contract or an agreement with God, has five parts:

If I was going to sell you a car, we would have to enter into an agreement. I would offer the contract, and I would promise to do something for you (in this case give you the car). Our agreement would have terms, what you would agree to do by entering into this agreement (in this case the terms would be to give me a certain amount of money.) If you agreed with the contract, you would accept it and we would sign a document. This document would be the sign of our agreement.

The five different parts of an agreement

Looking at these components helps us to understand the agreement that God offers us and how we can enter into peace with Him.

1) The initiator. The first component of an agreement is the person that offers it. Someone has to initiate and offer the agreement. The person who offers the agreement of peace with God is God Himself.

2) The recipient. The second component of an agreement is the person who receives the agreement. This is the person who accepts the agreement that the other offers. In terms of our agreement with God, every man and every woman who accepts the agreement enters into peace with God.

3) The promises. An agreement also has promises. This is what the person who offers the agreement offers to do for the person who enters into it.

4) The terms. The fourth element of an agreement is the terms. The terms are what the person who

offers the agreement asks the person who accepts the agreement to do.

5)   The sign. Finally, there is always a sign of the agreement. The sign is something physical that makes the agreement real.

A series of agreements

The history of God in the Bible is a series of agreements that God has offered to different people. Let's look at several of these agreements:

God's agreement with Adam

The first agreement that God offered was to Adam, the first man ever created. God offered him a paradise in the garden of Eden, and asked Adam to obey Him. As you probably know, Adam disobeyed God, breaking his agreement with God.

Hosea 6

7 *Like Adam, they have broken the covenant— they were unfaithful to me there.*

God's agreements with Noah

God offered two different agreements to Noah. First, He offered him salvation from the flood and He asked him to build the ark. Noah obeyed and entered into an agreement with God. Which is why God saved him.

Genesis 6

18 But I will establish my covenant with you, and you will enter the ark—you and your sons and your wife and your sons' wives with you.

After the flood, God established another agreement with Noah. He promised to never again flood the earth.

Genesis 9

9 "I now establish my covenant with you and with your descendants after you 10 and with every living creature that was with you—the birds, the livestock and all the wild animals, all those that came out of the ark with you—every living creature on earth. 11 I establish my covenant with you: Never again will all life be destroyed by the waters of a flood; never again will there be a flood to destroy the earth.

God's agreement with Abraham

Another agreement God offered was to Abraham. In Genesis 12-18, God offers to be the God of Abraham, to bless him, and to give him many offspring. What God asks of Abraham in this agreement is that Abraham obey Him.

Genesis 17

1 When Abram was ninety-nine years old, the LORD appeared to him and said, "I am God Almighty ; walk before me faithfully and be blameless. 2 Then I will make my covenant between me and you and will greatly increase your numbers." 3 Abram fell facedown, and God said to him, 4 "As for me, this is my covenant with you: You will be the father of many nations.

God's agreement with Israel

Later, God made an agreement with Abraham's grandson: Jacob (or Israel). This agreement wasn't just for Jacob, but was also for his descendants and lasted until Jesus died on the cross. In this agreement, God promises Jacob and his descendants that they will be his special nation, and He asks them to obey Him.

Exodus 19

5 Now if you obey me fully and keep my covenant, then out of all nations you will be my treasured possession.

Forgiveness in Jesus — the current agreement

Through the years, God has offered various agreements to men and women. Only those who have entered into an agreement with God experience peace with God.

The Bible teaches that when Jesus came and died on the cross, God established a new agreement or pact. Speaking of Jesus, the Bible says:

Hebrews 8

6 But in fact the ministry Jesus has received is as superior to theirs as the covenant of which he is mediator is superior

to the old one, since the new covenant is established on
better promises.

God offers the agreement

God is the one who offers this agreement. He takes the
initiative and offers us the option of entering into peace
with Himself.

He offers it to everyone

In spite of the fact that only those who have entered into this
agreement have peace with God, God offers the agreement
to everyone. Every person can enter into this agreement
and be at peace with God, but not every person does.

1 Timothy 2

4 (God,) who wants all people to be saved and to come to a
knowledge of the truth.

He promises forgiveness

Just like every other agreement, the agreement that God
offers contains promises.

To those who enter into this agreement, He promises
forgiveness from sin. Everyone who enters into this
agreement can cross the bridge from where they are, far
from Him, and receive forgiveness for each time they have
or will have disobeyed God.

Acts 2

38 Peter replied, "Repent and be baptized, every one of you, in the name of Jesus Christ for the forgiveness of your sins. And you will receive the gift of the Holy Spirit.

God also promises adoption into his family. This means that when someone enters into this agreement with God, He receives him or her as his child.

John 1

12 Yet to all who did receive him, to those who believed in his name, he gave the right to become children of God

Additionally, God promises eternal life at his side to each of his children.

Romans 6

23 For the wages of sin is death, but the gift of God is eternal life in Christ Jesus our Lord.

In this agreement, God promises much more than we deserve. He does this because He desperately wants us to be at peace with Him.

He asks for our obedience

The terms that God asks of each person who wants to enter into this agreement with Him is nothing more than obedience. He asks his children to live lives in obedience to Him.

1 John 2

6 Whoever claims to live in him must live as Jesus did.

Our obedience is not the condition for us to enter into the agreement. In other words, we don't have to be obedient to God before we can enter into peace with Him. What He asks is that his children live in obedience to Him after they enter into the agreement with Him.

1 John 3

8 The one who does what is sinful is of the devil, because the devil has been sinning from the beginning. The reason the Son of God appeared was to destroy the devil's work. 9 Those who are born of God will not continue to sin, because God's seed remains in them; they cannot go on sinning, because they have been born of God.

God's child doesn't have to be perfect. In fact, no one is perfect, but God asks that his children always make their best effort to disobey Him less and continually become more like Jesus.

Communion is a sign

One of the physical signs of the agreement between us and God is the Lord's Supper, or Communion. The reason that God's children regularly eat bread and drink grape juice or wine together is because Jesus said that this ceremony or meal would be a visible sign of the agreement that God would offer to everyone.

That is why Jesus said before he died:

Matthew 26

26 While they were eating, Jesus took bread, and when he had given thanks, he broke it and gave it to his disciples, saying, "Take and eat; this is my body." 27 Then he took the cup, and when he had given thanks, he gave it to them, saying, "Drink from it, all of you. 28 This is my blood of the covenant, which is poured out for many for the forgiveness of sins.

Every time we celebrate Communion, we remember the death of Christ, the agreement with God, and the forgiveness that his children have.

When someone decides to enter into this agreement, they have peace with God

Who has peace with God? Every person who has entered into this formal agreement with God.

That is why we can say that when someone decides to enter into this agreement, he or she immediately has peace with God.

In the next study, we will see how to make the decision to enter into this agreement with God.

What we've seen so far:

- We need peace with God...because we are separated from God. (Chapter 1)
- Jesus is the bridge to God. (Chapter 2)
- Only the person who has entered into an agreement with God has peace with God. (Chapter 3)

Chapter 4

Accepting Peace

Now, the key question is: "How do we enter into peace with God?" If Jesus and his cross is the bridge between us and God, how do we cross the bridge of Jesus' cross and get to God?

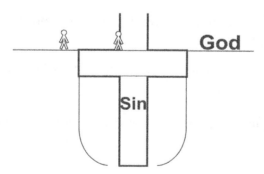

That is an important question, because there are many who know about Jesus, but don't have peace with God. In other words, just because a bridge exists for everyone, doesn't mean that everyone crosses it.

We try to be "close to God"

Many times we try to do different things in order to be close to God. We try different methods like:

- Going to church
- Stopping a particular sin
- Reading the Bible

We think that maybe by doing more of the things that we relate to God, He will accept us and we can get closer to Him.

This doesn't work

After trying to get close to God by doing things that we think He will like, we come to the conclusion that this is only making us more religious, and we still don't have peace with God.

- You can go to church for years and not feel close to God.

- You can clean up your life and still be far away from God.

So, the question persists: How can we enter into peace with God?

God offers us an agreement

In the last study, we saw how God offers an agreement or a covenant to every person. This agreement that God offers is the answer to the question of: "How can we be at peace with

God? Only a person who has entered into this agreement with God has peace with God.

The Invitation

The agreement that God offers is an invitation to be in peace with Him. It is a formal agreement that God offers to any person. When someone accepts the agreement, God promises total forgiveness of sin, or disobedience, and the adoption into his family as his dearly loved child. God also asks the person who enters into this agreement to promise Him submission and obedience.

You only have peace with God if you enter into this agreement with God

Even though God offers this agreement to everyone, only those who have decided to enter into this agreement have peace with God. Anyone who accepts the agreement that God offers, crosses over the bridge that is the forgiveness of Jesus, and enters into peace with God.

So, it is very important to ask the question: How can someone enter into this agreement with God?

Big Idea #4: You enter into the agreement with God when you say "yes"

In the Bible, in the book of Acts, a short time after Jesus ascended into heaven and left his followers with the task of talking about Him to the whole world, Peter, one of the first followers of Jesus, told the story of Jesus to a huge group of people.

After describing how everyone he is talking to is far from God, they asked: "What should we do?". In other words, they were asking how they could enter into peace with God.

Peter told them that they had to make a decision. He was telling them what they have to do to enter into the agreement with God and have peace with Him.

Acts 2

38 Peter replied, "Repent and be baptized, every one of you, in the name of Jesus Christ for the forgiveness of your sins. And you will receive the gift of the Holy Spirit.

You enter in a moment

What we see in the answer of Peter to those who asked "What shall we do?", is that you enter into peace with God in a single moment.

- It isn't something gradual
- You don't sign a contract in steps
- You can't be 80% decided

It is all or nothing. In one moment you are on one side of the canyon, far from God, with all of your sin separating you from God, and in the instant that you make this decision, you cross from one side to the other and you are at peace with God, forgiven of all your sins and now a daughter or son of God.

Do you have a moment?

Do you have a moment in which you decided to enter into peace with God, a moment in which you made a decision to return to God and were baptized? Have you experienced this moment?

To say "yes" means a lot

Even though it occurs in a moment, saying "yes" to God means a lot. It is a moment full of meaning, and in this moment something huge happens.

Saying "Yes" isn't something we do

Even though in this moment we make a decision and enter into an agreement with God, it is important that we emphasize here that it isn't something we do to earn our salvation. We don't earn the favor and the pardon of God when we make this decision. We are saved by the grace of God, not by what we do.

Ephesians 2

8 For it is by grace you have been saved, through faith-- and this not from yourselves, it is the gift of God-- 9 not by works, so that no one can boast.

Saying "Yes" is accepting

Making this decision to enter into an agreement with God is simply accepting the gift of eternal life and pardon from sin that God offers. It is saying "yes" to God and receiving the promise that you are now his son or daughter.

Saying "Yes" is entering

When someone makes this decision, he receives forgiveness and peace, and the Spirit of God comes and lives in him. By saying "yes", you enter into peace with God.

Acts 2

38 Peter replied, "Repent and be baptized, every one of you, in the name of Jesus Christ for the forgiveness of your sins. And you will receive the gift of the Holy Spirit.

You enter into the agreement when you say "yes" with everything you are

If this moment of saying "yes" to the offer of peace that God extends is so big and such an important moment, we really should look at how the Bible says the first followers of Christ made this decision.

What we see when we read the book of Acts and other books in the Bible, is that saying "yes" to the agreement with Christ means saying "yes" with everything you are, both soul and body. It is a complete decision that encompasses our entire life.

The Bible teaches and demonstrates that a person enters into peace with God when he says "yes" with his whole being: with his head, mouth, heart, and body.

Believing is saying "yes" with your head

In order to be able to say "yes" to God, you must have faith, or believe, in Jesus; you have to put all your trust in Him. You have to believe:

- That you need a savior
- That Jesus is the son of God
- That only Jesus can save you

Believing in Jesus is saying "yes" with your head. It is the first step to enter into peace with God. That is why Jesus said:

John 5

24 "Very truly I tell you, whoever hears my word and believes him who sent me has eternal life and will not be judged but has crossed over from death to life.

Repenting is saying "yes" with your heart

Saying "yes" with your heart is deciding that you desire to change. That you want to leave behind the life in which you made your own decisions, and enter into a life where you do your best to obey God in every area.

Acts 2

38 Peter replied, "Repent...

Repentance is turning to God. Before this moment of repentance, you were your own boss. You decided what to do, what to think, what to feel, and what to say. Many times you decided to do, feel, think, and say things that go against

God's will. In other words, you decided to disobey God. After repenting, you allow God to be the Boss of your life.

The two parts of repentance

The first part is recognizing and accepting that until this moment, you haven't lived how God wants you to live. Maybe you don't always disobey God, but many times you do. Repenting is saying: "I make my own decisions, and many times I have decided to disobey God."

The second part of repenting or saying "yes" with your heart is deciding that now God will be the Boss of your life. It's deciding that He will have authority over every area of your life: what you think, what you say, your family life, your friendships, your hobbies, your habits, your sex life — in other words, your whole life.

At this moment, you might not fully know what it means to obey God with your life. Saying "yes" with your heart is making the decision that it doesn't matter what God asks of you in the future, you will obey.

It doesn't mean that you have to be perfect after making this decision. It is nothing more than saying: "From now on, I will do my best to live as a child of God."

Confessing is saying "yes" with your mouth

Just like an agreement between two people, in order to enter into the agreement with God, you must first say, or confess with your mouth, that you believe in Jesus. You must also confess your desire to enter into this agreement with God.

It is necessary to verbally recognize the decision you are making.

Romans 10

9 If you declare with your mouth, "Jesus is Lord," and believe in your heart that God raised him from the dead, you will be saved. 10 For it is with your heart that you believe and are justified, and it is with your mouth that you profess your faith and are saved.

Being baptized is saying "yes" with your body

We seal our decision to enter into this agreement with God by being baptized. This is the moment when with our body, we tell God that: "I am deciding to completely surrender to You." The moment of being baptized is a very decisive moment.

Acts 2

38 Peter replied, "Repent and be baptized, every one of you, in the name of Jesus Christ for the forgiveness of your sins. And you will receive the gift of the Holy Spirit.

The word for "baptized" in the original Greek text means "to immerse". To be baptized, according to the Bible, means for your whole body to be completely immersed in water.

Also, when Peter describes baptism in this passage, he is speaking in the context of a decision made consciously by the person being baptized.

The moment of your baptism is when you finish the process of making your decision to be a child of God and enter into peace with God.

Where are you?

Bringing yourself to say "yes" is a process

As you can see, saying "yes" to God is a process. It starts in the mind by believing, then in the heart by deciding that you want to enter into this agreement with God, with our mouth we publicly confess our decision, and finally, we seal it with our baptism. Every part of this process is important, because by making this decision, we enter into peace with God.

Where are you in this process?

Now, the important question is: Where are you in this life-changing process of saying "yes" to God?

- Do you believe that you are separated from God because of your disobedience? Do you believe that Jesus Christ is God's Son and is Himself God? Do you believe that He died on the cross, paying the price for your sin? Do you want to be God's child? Do you want to put all of your trust in Jesus? When you do, you are saying "yes" with your mind.

- Do you accept that many times in your life you have decided to disobey God? Are you willing to decide that you will let God be the Boss of your life? When you do, you are saying "yes" with your heart.

- Are you prepared to tell your friends and family about your decision? When you do, you are saying "yes" with your mouth.

- Do you want to be baptized and seal your decision to become God's child? When you do, you are saying "yes" with your body.

Where are you in this process of deciding to enter into peace with God?

What is stopping you?

What is stopping you from taking the next step and sealing your decision to become God's child? Let's look at some of the statements people make in regards to why they don't take the step of entering into peace with God.

Statement

"I don't know enough about God and the Bible."

Reality

The reality is that you never will know everything there is to know about God. What is important is to obey what you already know. If you know how to enter into peace with God, He expects you to obey. Then you will continue to learn more about God and his will.

Statement

"I need to change my life first."

Reality

The reality is that you will never be good enough to be worthy to enter into peace with God. Remember, the reason that you need forgiveness is that you aren't perfect, but God accepts you just as you are. He wants to forgive you. Not because you change your life first, but because Jesus died and paid the price for your sin.

After deciding to become a child of God, He will help you as you continue changing things in your life. From then on, you will make changes with the help of the Spirit of God.

Statement

"I don't know if I will be able to continue once I start."

Reality

The reality is that on one hand it isn't easy to live life as a child of God. It is a big change and many who have made that decision eventually stop following God.

On the other hand, when you decide to become God's child, the Spirit of God guides you and helps you. You aren't alone in this new life. God will give you everything that you need in order to continue following.

Statement

"I don't need to do this, I was already baptized when I was a baby."

Reality

The decision to follow Jesus is more than a decision to be baptized. In the Bible, the decision to enter into peace with God is a decision that you must make for yourself, and that only a person with the use of his own reason can make. You must believe in Jesus, decide in your heart to turn to God, accept that God will be your Boss, tell others about this decision and be baptized by immersion in water. A baby can't do this. If your parents baptized you as a baby, they did it because they love you and wanted the best for you. However, what they did for you was not your own decision, and God asks everyone to make their own decision.

Statement

"I have already accepted Jesus in my heart."

"I was baptized, but I wasn't making the decision to accept Jesus as my Lord and Saviour and to follow Him with my whole life."

"I was baptized, but not as part of making my decision to follow Jesus."

Reality

In our day, the decision to follow Jesus is commonly abbreviated. Sometimes this decision is abbreviated by omitting baptism, and focusing entirely on repentance. When this happens, the person making the decision is rightly encouraged to make a mental and heart decision to surrender to the lordship of Christ, however this decision isn't sealed with baptism. Frequently the person will be immersed in water in a ceremony at a later date, but this immersion isn't part of making his decision to surrender to Jesus.

Other times, this decision is abbreviated by omitting repentance, and reducing the decision to just baptism. In this scenario, baptism is seen as a sort of magic ritual that imparts salvation.

There is a verse in 1 Peter that can help us know what we should do when this has been our experience.

1 Peter 3:21

21 Baptism, which corresponds to this, now saves you, not as a removal of dirt from the body but as an appeal to God for a good conscience, through the resurrection of Jesus Christ,

We see two important truths in this verse: First, baptism is an essential part of making the decision to follow Jesus. Just as in Acts 2:38, this verse teaches us that one cannot make the decision to surrender to Jesus without being baptized. The second truth that we see in this verse is that being immersed in water only has spiritual significance within the context of making the decision to follow Jesus. That is to say, without being accompanied by the heart decision to surrender to the lordship of Christ, it isn't baptism.

So then, if you have made the decision to surrender to Jesus in your heart but have never been baptized, you haven't made the complete decision that Jesus asks of you. You need to seal your decision to follow Jesus by being baptized.

If you were baptized after and separate from making the decision to surrender to Jesus in your heart, then the verse from 1 Peter 3:21 applies directly to you. Your immersion was a ceremony, but since it wasn't part of you making your decision to follow Jesus, it wasn't biblical baptism. You need to seal your decision to follow Jesus by being baptized as part of making this decision.

If you were baptized but you weren't making the decision in your heart to follow Jesus and completely surrender to Him, then you need to make the decision to follow Christ and surrender to Jesus, accepting Him as your Lord and Savior by repenting (making the decision in your heart) and by being baptized (sealing this decision by being immersed in water).

What is keeping you from making your decision today?

At any moment you can decide that you want to enter into peace with God. At any time of the day or night you can turn to God in your heart, and through baptism enter into the agreement or covenant with God.

It must be your own decision and you have to make it when you are ready. I can't encourage you enough to not wait too long to make this decision. The most important thing in life is to become God's child.

Mark 16

16 Whoever believes and is baptized will be saved, but whoever does not believe will be condemned.

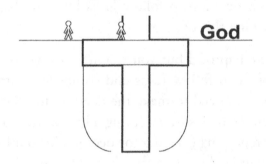

What we've seen so far:

- We need peace with God...because we are separated from God. (Chapter 1)

- Jesus is the bridge to God. (Chapter 2)

- Only the person who has entered into an agreement with God has peace with God. (Chapter 3)

- You enter into the agreement with God when you say "yes" with your whole being. (Chapter 4)

Chapter 5

What Jesus Asks from You

When we feel far from God, our temptation is to try to add a little bit of God to our lives. We go to church more, read the Bible, or try to stop a bad habit or a sin we have.

So, when we think about the decision to turn to God and be baptized, it would be easy to think of it in religious terms. In other words, to think that you are "joining a religion." It would be easy to think that you are doing something that will simply provide you with forgiveness and that's it; that you are adding a little bit of God to your life so that everything works out well.

I want to discourage you from thinking like this. If you are thinking of turning to God and being baptized, the decision that you are contemplating is much bigger than just getting into water and joining a religion. God, in his Word, says that this is a decision to give Him your whole life, to completely give yourself to Him and to his lordship.

I don't say this to scare you off or to cause you to not want to make this decision. Instead, my desire is to help you think through the decision so that when you decide to get baptized, the decision that you are making is in fact the decision that God asks of you, and that by making this decision you can enter into peace with God.

It's a question of loyalty

What God really wants from us when we come to Him and desire to enter into peace and forgiveness, is our loyalty.

God desires our loyalty

When someone asked Jesus what the greatest commandment was, He answered by saying that God wants our love.

Matthew 22

37 Jesus answered: Love the Lord your God with all your heart, soul, and mind. 38 This is the first and most important commandment.

God tells each of us to love Him with everything we are and to submit ourselves to Him. In other words, Jesus explains that what God really demands from his children is their loyalty.

It makes sense that this kind of absolute surrender is what God would want from his children. He is the only God. He is all-powerful. He knows everything. He can do whatever He wants. We are his creation. He made us. This is why He demands our complete surrender to Him and to his will.

In spite of the fact that this is what God wants from us, this is not how we normally live. We typically choose to be loyal to other things in our lives, and as a result, we surrender our passion, energy, and obedience to them.

We are loyal to many things in our lives

We give our loyalty to many different things. Ironically, we are not nearly as loyal to the God who made us, as we are to so many other things in life.

Some people are loyal to vices or habits — like drinking too much alcohol or using drugs. This loyalty can be seen when someone sacrifices his life (family, money, time, friends, and health) in order to pursue these habits.

Others are loyal to their possessions. For these people the most important thing in life is what they have acquired and what they are planning on buying. They are always thinking about the next purchase, the next time they can go shopping, about having something better, or the next thing they are going to buy. They give their time, energy and money to accumulating possessions.

Other people are more loyal to their family than anything else in life. What the family wants and demands comes first. Even though family is very important, sometimes one can give all of their loyalty to their family and make it the center of their life.

Some people are loyal to earning and accumulating money. Their life revolves around what they can earn, and they are only focused on earning more. Of course, it is necessary to earn money to live, but there is a temptation to let earning money consume our life.

Where you put your loyalty determines how you live

We are all loyal to different things, but all of us are alike in this: our lives are controlled by the things to which we give our loyalty.

The object of our loyalty determines three essential areas of life:

1) It demands obedience

When we give our loyalty to something — whether to family, alcohol, friends, making money, or anything else, we are saying that we will obey the demands it puts on us. Since we are loyal to it, we obey it.

2) It gives purpose

Whatever we are loyal to brings purpose into our lives. It gives us something to live for. Even though that purpose might only be getting to the end of the week to be able to go out drinking or shopping, this does give some sort of purpose to life. The object of our loyalty gives us purpose.

3) It produces joy

Whatever we are loyal to produces a kind of temporary joy in us. If we give our loyalty, for example, to going shopping and accumulating things, then each time we are able to go shopping and buy something new, we feel joy. Our loyalty produces joy in us.

Our loyalty

The question for each of us is: What are am I loyal to in my life? At times it is hard to know what we are loyal to because it becomes a part of who we are and we don't even realize that it is our master. There are some questions that we can ask ourselves that can help us see the object of our loyalty:

Loyalty questions

- What is the most important thing in my life?
- What do I have in my life that motivates the things that I do with my time and money?
- What do I anticipate and desire?
- What do I think about a lot?
- What do I fear losing?

Now can we answer the question: What am I loyal to?

The center

Where we put our loyalty determines what is at the center of our life. You can know what you are loyal to by looking at what is at the center of your life. What do you obey? What gives you purpose in life? What produces joy in your life?

God wants to be in the center

The reason that Jesus said that the most important commandment is to love God above everything else — with heart, soul, and mind —, is because God wants — actually, He demands — to be at the center of his children's lives.

This is why the decision to follow God and be baptized is a decision of loyalty.

Big Idea #5: In order to enter into peace with God, you must decide give Him all your loyalty

It is relatively easy to be religious. You just have to attend church semi-regularly, avoid certain sins, hide the sins you can't shake, and participate in some rituals (like baptism or communion.)

However, it is extremely difficult to give our loyalty to God. Because of this, during his life Jesus emphasized many times that God doesn't want people to do more religious works, rather He desires people who give Him all of their loyalty.

Jesus asks for a radical decision

Lukes 14

25 Now great crowds accompanied him, and he turned and said to them, 26 "If anyone comes to me and does not hate his own father and mother and wife and children and brothers and sisters, yes, and even his own life, he cannot be my disciple. 27 Whoever does not bear his own cross and come after me cannot be my disciple.

To decide to follow Jesus is to decide to move your loyalty from where it is now, and give it to God. It is making the decision that God will be at the center of your life; that while you won't be perfect, you will be totally surrendered to Him in your mind, heart, and soul.

The decision to follow God is a decision to give Him your loyalty

It is a decision that for the rest of your life, Jesus will be your Lord. That following Him will be the most important thing for you. That your new identity will be that of God's child. That obeying your new Father will be your highest priority.

That is the decision that Jesus asks us to make: to give God our loyalty.

What does it mean to give our loyalty to God?

Giving our loyalty to God means focusing our life on God and on his desires and purposes. It means putting God in the center of our life.

We give obedience

Giving our loyalty to God means that we decide that we will obey God. No one ever does this perfectly, but putting God in the center of our life is deciding that we will do the best we can to obey Him.

I Want Peace with God

We receive purpose

Giving our loyalty to God brings purpose to our life. Now our purpose comes from being with God, from reading his word and from doing his work on this earth.

We find joy

Finally, giving our loyalty to God produces joy. Obeying and serving God produces joy in the life of God's child. The reason for this joy is that now we are doing what is pleasing to our Father, and this produces an indescribable joy and peace in our heart, soul and mind. This joy isn't temporary, like the joy that at times we experience when other things in life give us joy. The joy that comes from knowing God as our Father, and obeying and serving Him is a joy that truly satisfies and never leaves us.

The decision

Now, if you are thinking of entering into peace with God by turning to Him and being baptized, you have to think through this decision. Because the decision that is in front of you isn't just if you are going to participate in a religious ritual, but rather if you are ready to give all your loyalty to God.

What is the cost?

On one occasion when Jesus talked about this idea of loyalty, He used two examples to demonstrate that it is very important to be conscious of the decision that one is making when deciding to follow Him:

78

Luke 14

28 Suppose one of you wants to build a tower. What is the first thing you will do? Won't you sit down and figure out how much it will cost and if you have enough money to pay for it? 29 Otherwise, you will start building the tower, but not be able to finish. Then everyone who sees what is happening will laugh at you. 30 They will say, "You started building, but could not finish the job." 31 What will a king do if he has only ten thousand soldiers to defend himself against a king who is about to attack him with twenty thousand soldiers? 32 Before he goes out to battle, won't he first sit down and decide if he can win? If he thinks he won't be able to defend himself, he will send messengers and ask for peace while the other king is still a long way off.

Are you willing to give all of your loyalty to God? You don't have to be perfect after making this decision, there will always be areas of your life in which you won't obey God perfectly, but giving Him your loyalty is saying: "I commit to following and obeying God the best that I am able. He will be my Lord."

What would you have to change?

What would you have to change in your life if you decided to give all your loyalty to God? It might be better to ask the question like this: In what areas of your life are you currently not living in obedience to God?

Deciding to give all your loyalty to God means deciding to surrender those areas of your life to Him. You don't have to completely change before making your decision by repenting and being baptized, but you do have to decide that, with God's help, after making your decision, you will obey God in these — and all other — areas of your life.

The decision you would be making is to accept that Jesus would be your Lord; that He would govern your life; that whatever He told you to do, you would do; that He would have all of your loyalty. Jesus finishes this text by saying:

Luke 14

33 So therefore, any one of you who does not renounce all that he has cannot be my disciple.

When you decide, God gives you life

When you decide to give your loyalty to God, He gives you life. God doesn't take good things away from us, rather He gives us true life. He desires to give us life, but He knows that only when we give Him our loyalty, can we truly enter into life.

That's why Jesus said:

John 10

10 The thief comes only to steal and kill and destroy. I came that they may have life and have it abundantly.

True life

The life that Jesus has for us is a life full of joy and purpose. It is a perfect life with God for all eternity. We enter into that life by deciding to become children of God, leave everything else that has our loyalty, and give our loyalty completely to God.

Luke 9

23 Then Jesus said to all the people: If any of you want to be my followers, you must forget about yourself. You must take up your cross each day and follow me. 24 If you want to save your life, you will destroy it. But if you give up your life for me, you will save it. 25 What will you gain, if you own the whole world but destroy yourself or waste your life?

You should make this decision

I would encourage you to make the decision to give your life to Jesus and enter into peace with God. It is a decision to completely turn to God and to give Him your loyalty that you make by repenting and being baptized. When you make this decision, you receive total forgiveness from all your sins — past and future, and you receive the Spirit of God who will be with you every moment and who will guide you in this new life. You will be a child of God.

Acts 2

38 Peter replied, "Repent and be baptized, every one of you, in the name of Jesus Christ for the forgiveness of your sins. And you will receive the gift of the Holy Spirit.

What we've seen so far:

- We need peace with God...because we are separated from God. (Chapter 1)
- Jesus is the bridge to God. (Chapter 2)
- Only the person who has entered into an agreement with God has peace with God. (Chapter 3)
- You enter into the agreement with God when you say "yes" with your whole being. (Chapter 4)
- In order to enter into peace with God, you must decide give Him all your loyalty (Chapter 5)

Chapter 6

Living in Peace

Our life completely changes in the moment when we make the decision to enter into peace with God: we are transformed and forgiven; we find life and love; God adopts us and we receive his Spirit. However, we are left with a question: How do I live the rest of my life in peace with God? How should we live after that moment, after that decision? That is an important question. Since we probably have more years of life in front of us, and now that we are God's children, we need to know how a child of God should live.

How do I live afterwards?

We know how we lived before. We know that many times our past life wasn't pleasing to God. We did, thought and said things that were sins. So our old way of living and talking and thinking isn't going to be pleasing to God now.

It is as if we have to encounter a totally different way of living. And that isn't easy.

We struggle to live as children of God

It can be hard to live as God's child. Any person that has tried, knows first hand that it isn't easy. It is difficult for two reasons:

First, it is difficult to live as God's child because we are used to how we lived before, and we really don't know how to live differently.

The second reason that it is difficult to live as children of God is that being God's child can many times take us to one of two dangerous extremes.

Two extremes

God's children have the tendency to go to one of two extremes in their personal life. We know that God saves us and makes us his children, and this knowledge can make some of us go to one extreme in our life and others go to the opposite extreme. Neither of these two extremes is pleasing to God.

What are these two extremes?

Extreme number one: licentiousness

Licentiousness is basically saying: "I can do what I want, when I want; God has forgiven me and will continue to forgive me." It doesn't matter how I live, I'm not going to hell because Jesus paid the price for my sin." It's thinking that: "God loves me and has grace and patience with me. I am not perfect and He will always love me, so there aren't any limits to what I can do."

It is easy to go to the extreme of licentiousness because all of this, in part, is true. It is true that God forgives his children of every sin, that He always loves them, that He has patience with his children, and that they won't spend eternity in hell.

However, the part of this extreme that isn't true is saying or thinking that if God has forgiven you, then you can live however you want. The Bible says time after time that this is not true.

Galatians 5

13 You, my brothers and sisters, were called to be free. But do not use your freedom to indulge the sinful nature ; rather, serve one another humbly in love.

Extreme number two: continual condemnation

Continual condemnation is a cycle. It starts by trying to obey God, failing and committing a sin, feeling that you aren't worth anything and are not okay with God, and then trying to obey more, failing again, feeling worse, etc. It is like a snowball that rolls down a mountain, and grows and grows and grows.

This condemnation comes from the idea that when I do something I shouldn't, then things are not okay between God and I, but when I behave, then things are okay between us. It is feeling that I am only at peace with God — saved and forgiven —, in those moments when I don't sin. When

I say a bad word, think a bad thought, or do something I shouldn't, then I am not okay with God, and in that moment, I am probably not saved.

When we live with this idea, we invariably end up feeling a huge amount of guilt and condemnation. No one is perfect, not even the person who has been God's child for many years. If we believe that we are only okay with God when we don't sin, then every day we experience moments when we feel that we are not okay with God, because we sin everyday. In these moments we feel condemned, guilty, and like spiritual failures.

What is your tendency?

To which of these two extremes do you have the tendency to go?

Do you have the tendency to tolerate sin in your life? Do you feel confident in your relationship with God because you made your decision to follow Him, but now you don't worry at all about your obedience? It could be that your tendency is towards licentiousness.

On the other hand, do you feel like a spiritual loser every time you commit a sin? Do you feel destroyed when you say or do or think something you shouldn't? Do you feel that many times you aren't at peace with God because of the things you do? It could be that your tendency is towards continual condemnation.

We don't truly understand what it means to be a child of God

It is difficult for us to live as children of God and we tend to go toward one of the two extremes because it is difficult for us to truly understand what it means to be God's child. Many times, we only see a part of the life that God has for us.

The reality is that being God's son or daughter has two components. In order to live as a child of God, it is necessary to understand both.

Big Idea #6: Being God's child brings security and changes

Security and changes are the two parts of our identity as children of God. One is fixed while the other one is variable. We get into trouble in our Christian life when we don't acknowledge these two parts of our identity as children of God.

Part 1 — Security

When someone makes a decision to enter into peace with God, he or she is instantly made a son or daughter of God. At that moment, God adopts us as his children. We are forgiven and cleansed from all sin that we have committed in the past and all future sin. We enter into a secure state that we receive by God's grace, not by our good behavior.

Galatians 3

26 All of you are God's children because of your faith in Christ Jesus.

By not acknowledging the security that comes with being God's child, many of God's children go to the extreme of feeling continual condemnation. God doesn't accept us only when we behave, He accepts us when we enter into the agreement with Him. At that moment, He forgives us and makes us his children.

When a person is at peace with God, he is a child of God. That is a constant reality. It doesn't depend on his moment by moment behavior.

Fixed state

Even though we sometimes feel that our standing with God changes according to our behavior, being a child of God is a fixed state. It doesn't change from one moment to the next.

2 Corinthians 5

17 Therefore, if anyone is in Christ, the new creation has come: The old has gone, the new is here!

This doesn't change from one moment to another; the child of God is new, he is different, he has been transformed.

Like a car

Being God's child brings security because it is a state. It is similar to a car's motor. A car's motor can be turned on or off, but it can't be half-way on. It is the same way with a child of God. He is totally —100% ☒— a child of God. He can't be half a child of God. A child of God, even though imperfect, is 100% a child of God.

It doesn't change (unless you leave Him)

There is so much security in being a child of God because God promises that his sons and daughters are at peace with Him, that they have forgiveness, and they have eternal life.

1 John 5

13 I write these things to you who believe in the name of the Son of God so that you may know that you have eternal life.

It is possible to leave God, but it doesn't happen because you mess up and commit a sin. The only way to stop being God's child is to decide to leave your Father.

1 Timoteo 1

18 Timothy, my son, I give you this instruction in keeping with the prophecies once made about you, so that by following them you may fight the good fight, 19 holding on to faith and a good conscience. Some have rejected these and so have shipwrecked their faith.

Matthew 24

13 but whoever stands firm to the end will be saved.

Sadly, there are people who decide to not continue in their relationship with God. They decide to return to living in rebellion against God. However, unless you decide to leave God, you have security in your salvation.

Totally forgiven

The reason that God's child can be totally secure, in spite of not being perfect, is because God forgives his children's sin.

Acts 2

38 Peter replied, "Repent and be baptized, every one of you, in the name of Jesus Christ for the forgiveness of your sins. And you will receive the gift of the Holy Spirit.

Ephesians 1

4 For he chose us in him before the creation of the world to be holy and blameless in his sight. {...}

Being God's child doesn't mean that you receive forgiveness for past sins and then have to be perfect. God's forgiveness cleanses us from all of our sin, even sin we commit after deciding to become God's child. God forgives his children's past and future sins.

By grace

Obviously, this forgiveness isn't something that we deserve. If it seems weird to you that God would forgive his children of all their sin and would love them even when they don't behave perfectly, it's because it is strange that the King of the universe would forgive the rebellion against Himself by those He created.

The Bible says that God has grace and gives us forgiveness even though we don't deserve it. It is by this grace that we are saved.

Ephesians 2

8 For it is by grace you have been saved, through faith— and this is not from yourselves, it is the gift of God—

Even though this doesn't make sense to us, God's grace gives us security when we aren't perfect, because we understand that He saves us, loves us, and forgives us because He is our Father.

Security removes the continual condemnation

When God's child truly starts to understand the security that he has with his father, God, he experiences freedom from the continual condemnation that before held him captive in his mind and soul. When he understands that God loves, forgives and is his Father in spite of his imperfections, he can start to always feel at peace with God.

The Bible says that there is no condemnation for anyone who is God's child.`

Romans 8

1 Therefore, there is now no condemnation for those who are in Christ Jesus,

Part 2 — Changes

Being a child of God doesn't just bring security, it also brings changes. It's a life of complete security, in spite of our imperfections, while at the same time always letting God change and perfect us.

1 Peter 2

2 Like newborn babies, crave pure spiritual milk, so that by it you may grow up in your salvation,

It's a process

The state of God's child is fixed and secure, God accepts him in spite of his imperfections. At the same time, God always asks his children to be in a continual process of maturing, of changing, of leaving sin, and of becoming more like Jesus.

Ephesians 4

22 You were taught, with regard to your former way of life, to put off your old self, which is being corrupted by its deceitful desires;

Like a "clean" room

The life of God's child is something like many teenagers' bedrooms. Even though her room isn't ever completely clean, each day her mom or dad asks her to clean up her room, and every day she makes an effort to clean up. Day after day, little by little, her room gets a little bit more orderly. It may never be perfect, but the way her room looks when she is twenty should be much better than when she was fourteen.

That is how it is with God's children. Each day God asks them to change something, to leave another sin, to clean up their vocabulary, to stop thinking some impure thoughts, to change something ugly in their character. They never achieve perfection, but God always asks for one more change.

Ephesians 5

15 Be very careful, then, how you live—not as unwise but as wise,

The goal of these changes is that we become more like Jesus, who lived a perfect life.

Always imperfect

In the eyes of God, his children are perfect because they have been forgiven by the blood of Christ and covered with the perfection of Jesus's life. However, in reality we never live perfect lives. Even the great apostle Paul said that he wasn't perfect:

Philippians 3

12 Not that I have already obtained all this, or have already arrived at my goal, but I press on to take hold of that for which Christ Jesus took hold of me. 13 Brothers and sisters, I do not consider myself yet to have taken hold of it. {...}

The idea that being God's child brings change means that our external transformation doesn't take place overnight. Because of this, it is okay that we aren't perfect, but it isn't okay that we stay like we are.

Always changing

Paul ends this passage in Philippians 3 by saying that even though he isn't perfect, he goes forward, letting God change him each day and trying to become more like Jesus:

Philippians 3

13 Brothers and sisters, I do not consider myself yet to have taken hold of it. But one thing I do: Forgetting what is behind and straining toward what is ahead, 14 I press on toward the goal to win the prize for which God has called me heavenward in Christ Jesus.

The life as a child of God is a life of constant changes. God knows that his children aren't going to be perfect, but He desires that they are always striving for perfection, always leaving behind sins, always changing their character, always living lives that are more and more pure.

Philippians 1

6 being confident of this, that he who began a good work in you will carry it on to completion until the day of Christ Jesus.

The motivation

As we live in this process of continual change, it is really, really important to know the motivation behind our changes. We don't change our life and our character so that God will love us more or in order to earn his salvation and forgiveness. Remember, if someone is a child of God, he or she already has the complete security of being forgiven and saved.

The reason we change a little bit every day is because we are children of God and we want to act like children of God, we want to imitate our Father and become like Jesus.

Colossians 2

6 So then, just as you received Christ Jesus as Lord, continue to live your lives in him,

Constant changes protects us from licentiousness

When God's child accepts the fact that his Father wants him to always be changing, then he doesn't fall into licentiousness. He doesn't think that just because he is forgiven, he can live however he chooses. Instead, he understand that because he is God's son, he must live as a child of God.

1 John 2

6 Whoever claims to live in him must live as Jesus did.

If we accept the security that comes with being God's child and the constant changes that God desires to see in his children, then it would be helpful to look at the answer a very practical question:

What should I do when I sin?

What should I do in the moment when I realize that I used words I shouldn't have, that I lied, that I gossiped, that I thought a bad thought, or that I did something I shouldn't have done?

Remember, God's child is secure, he won't lose his salvation for having committed that sin. At the same time, God isn't happy when we sin, because our sin is rebellion against Him. He doesn't want us to make a habit of any sin. So, God asks his children to change when they sin.

So, what should God's child do when he sins? The Bible explains exactly how we should treat the sin that we see in our lives:

1 John 1

7 But if we walk in the light, as he is in the light, we have fellowship with one another, and the blood of Jesus, his Son, purifies us from all sin. 8 If we claim to be without sin, we deceive ourselves and the truth is not in us. 9 If we confess our sins, he is faithful and just and will forgive us our sins and purify us from all unrighteousness.

God says in his Word that we should always follow these steps when we sin:

1) Recognize our sin: Realize when we have done something that is displeasing to God.

2) Confess our sin: Tell God that we have sinned. We do this not so that He knows — He already knows what we have done before we confess. We confess our sin to God as a way of accepting that we have disobeyed Him.

3) Turn from the sin: God asks that when we realize we have sinned, we don't let that sin become a habit. He asks us to immediately leave this sin behind.

Can you make a habit of doing this every time you sin? When you do, you will be constantly changing to become more and more like Jesus.

Appendix

Summary Handouts

The best way to end each study is to give a page that summarizes the study to the person you are studying with. You could say something along the lines of: "I am going to leave this summary of what we just studied. If you would like, you can look it over and we can start our next study by talking about any question you might have."

The following are summary sheets for each study that you can feel free to photocopy and give to the people you study with.

Summary of Chapter 1

We Need Peace

The Big Question: Why don't I feel at peace with God?

The Big Idea: We need peace with God, because we are separated from God

The reason that many times we feel that we don't have peace with God is because we all disobey God. We do things that God prohibits, and we don't do good things that God asks us to do. Every time we disobey God, we sin. God has said in his word that our sin, or disobedience, separates us from Him. Additionally, God has promised to punish every disobedience with eternal death. This reality awakens a need within us to be at peace with God.

The Bible Says

Romans 3

23 for all have sinned and fall short of the glory of God,

Isaiah 59

1 Surely the arm of the LORD is not too short to save, nor his ear too dull to hear. 2 But your iniquities have separated you from your God; your sins have hidden his face from you, so that he will not hear. 3 For your hands are stained with blood, your fingers with guilt. Your lips have spoken lies, and your tongue mutters wicked things.

Romans 6

23 For the wages of sin is death, but the gift of God is eternal life in Christ Jesus our Lord.

Colossians 1

21 Once you were alienated from God and were enemies in your minds because of your evil behavior.

Ephesians 2

3 All of us also lived among them at one time, gratifying the cravings of our sinful nature and following its desires and thoughts. Like the rest, we were by nature objects of wrath.

Summary of Chapter 2

The Bridge to Peace

The Big Question: How can I have peace with God?

The Big Idea: Jesus is the bridge to God

Because of our disobedience, we do not have peace with God, but Jesus Christ, the Son of God, came into this world to pay the price of the punishment of our sin. Jesus lived a perfect life and died a cruel death that He did not deserve. In this way, He is able to offer forgiveness of sins to every person. You could say that Jesus is the bridge between us and God, and provides a path so that we can enter into peace with God.

The Bible Says

Romans 6

23 For the wages of sin is death,

1 Corinthians 15

1Now, brothers, I want to remind you of the gospel I preached to you, which you received and on which you have taken your stand.

3 For what I received I passed on to you as of first importance: that Christ died for our sins according to the Scriptures, 4 that he was buried, that he was raised on the third day according to the Scriptures,

John 14

6 Jesus answered, "I am the way and the truth and the life. No one comes to the Father except through me.

1 Peter 2

24 He himself bore our sins in his body on the tree, so that we might die to sins and live for righteousness; by his wounds you have been healed.

1 John 2

2 He is the atoning sacrifice for our sins, and not only for ours but also for the sins of the whole world.

1 John 5

12 He who has the Son has life; he who does not have the Son of God does not have life.

Ephesians 2

4 But because of his great love for us, God, who is rich in mercy, 5made us alive with Christ even when we were dead in transgressions—it is by grace you have been saved.

Romans 5

1 Therefore, since we have been justified through faith, we have peace with God through our Lord Jesus Christ,

Summary of Chapter 3

Peace & Covenants

The Big Question: Who has peace with God?

The Big Idea: Only the person who has entered into an agreement with God has peace with God

Jesus paid the price of the punishment of the sins of the entire world, but that doesn't mean that everyone has forgiveness and peace with God. Everyone has the option to enter into peace with God because of what Jesus did. However, the Bible teaches that only those who actually enter into a formal agreement, or covenant, with God have peace with God. Through his death, Jesus established an agreement or covenant with God that is offered to every person. It is an agreement in which God promises forgiveness and peace, and the person who enters into the agreement promises God his loyalty and obedience. Only those people who have made the decision to enter into this agreement with God have peace with God.

The Bible Says

Matthew 26

26 While they were eating, Jesus took bread, and when he had given thanks, he broke it and gave it to his disciples, saying, "Take and eat; this is my body." 27 Then he took the cup, and when he had given thanks, he gave it to them, saying, "Drink from it, all of you. 28 This is my blood of the covenant, which is poured out for many for the forgiveness of sins.

Hebrews 8

6 But in fact the ministry Jesus has received is as superior to theirs as the covenant of which he is mediator is superior to the old one, since the new covenant is established on better promises.

1 Timoteo 2

4 who wants all people to be saved and to come to a knowledge of the truth.

John 1

12 Yet to all who did receive him, to those who believed in his name, he gave the right to become children of God

1 John 2

6 Whoever claims to live in him must live as Jesus did.

Summary of Chapter 4

Accepting Peace

The Big Question: How can I enter into peace with God?

The Big Idea: You enter into the agreement with God when you say "yes"

You enter into peace with God in the moment in which you make a very specific decision. It is the decision to follow Jesus, to enter into a life-long agreement with God. You make this decision by saying "yes" to God with your whole being. You say yes with your whole being by believing in Jesus with your mind, confessing your desire to follow Him with your mouth, deciding in your heart that you will submit your will to God and that you will do your best to obey Him, and by being baptized, which is being completely immersed into water. At the moment you make this decision, you enter into peace with God, you receive forgiveness of your all sins — both past and future, and God makes you his child.

The Bible Says

John 5

24 "Very truly I tell you, whoever hears my word and believes him who sent me has eternal life and will not be judged but has crossed over from death to life.

Romans 10

9 If you declare with your mouth, "Jesus is Lord," and believe in your heart that God raised him from the dead, you will be saved. 10 For it is with your heart that you believe and are justified, and it is with your mouth that you profess your faith and are saved.

Mark 16

16 Whoever believes and is baptized will be saved, but whoever does not believe will be condemned.

Acts 2

38 Peter replied, "Repent and be baptized, every one of you, in the name of Jesus Christ for the forgiveness of your sins. And you will receive the gift of the Holy Spirit.

Summary of Chapter 5

What Jesus wants from us

The Big Question: What does Jesus want from me?

The Big Idea: Deciding to enter into peace with God is deciding to give Him your loyalty

It is easy to think that when we enter into peace with God, we are merely "adding a little bit of God to our lives." The reality is that when we come to Christ and desire to enter into peace with God, Christ wants something from us. What Jesus ask from us in the moment we decide to enter into peace with God is our loyalty. He wants to be our Lord and the center of our lives. The decision to enter into peace with God is to decide to give Him our loyalty.

The Bible Says

Matthew 22

37 Jesus answered: Love the Lord your God with all your heart, soul, and mind. 38 This is the first and most important commandment.

Luke 14

25 Now great crowds accompanied him, and he turned and said to them, 26 "If anyone comes to me and does not hate his own father and mother and wife and children and brothers and sisters, yes, and even his own life, he cannot be my disciple. 27 Whoever does not bear his own cross and come after me cannot be my disciple. 28 Suppose one of you wants to build a tower. What is the first thing you will do? Won't you sit down and figure out how much it will cost and if you have enough money to pay for it? 29 Otherwise, you will start building the tower, but not be able to finish. Then everyone who sees what is happening will laugh at you. 30 They will say, "You started building, but could not finish the job." 31 What will a king do if he has only ten thousand soldiers to defend himself against a king who is about to attack him with twenty thousand soldiers? 32 Before he goes out to battle, won't he first sit down and decide if he can win? If he thinks he won't be able to defend himself, he will send messengers and ask for peace while the other king is still a long way off. 33 So therefore, any one of you who does not renounce all that he has cannot be my disciple.

Lucas 9

23 Then Jesus said to all the people: If any of you want to be my followers, you must forget about yourself. You must take up your cross each day and follow me. 24 If you want to save your life, you will destroy it. But if you give up your life for me, you will save it. 25 What will you gain, if you own the whole world but destroy yourself or waste your life?

Acts 2

38 Peter replied, "Repent and be baptized, every one of you, in the name of Jesus Christ for the forgiveness of your sins. And you will receive the gift of the Holy Spirit.

Summary of Chapter 6

Living in Peace

The Big Question: How do I live after I enter into peace with God?

The Big Idea: Being God's child brings security and changes

It can be hard to live as a child of God. On one hand, the forgiveness we receive from God can sometimes make us feel that we can live however we want. On the other hand, when we don't live up to our commitment to obey God, we feel condemned and far from God.

The reality is that living as a child of God is made up of two parts. Being God's child means living a life of continual changes. In other words, God asks his children to always be fighting against the disobedience, or sin, in their lives. At the same time, He helps us to change and become more obedient.

The other part of what it means to be God's child is to live in the reality that in this life we will never be perfect. We will make mistakes. Some sins will be hard for us to give up. It is for this reason that being a child of God also means that we have security. God promises to forgive his children's sins. As long as we do not leave Him, He forgives our sins and helps us in our weaknesses.

The Bible Says

Galatians 5

13 You, my brothers and sisters, were called to be free. But do not use your freedom to indulge the sinful nature ; rather, serve one another humbly in love.

1 John 5

13 I write these things to you who believe in the name of the Son of God so that you may know that you have eternal life.

Matthew 24

13 but whoever stands firm to the end will be saved.

Ephesians 2

8 For it is by grace you have been saved, through faith— and this is not from yourselves, it is the gift of God—

Ephesians 1

4 For he chose us in him before the creation of the world to be holy and blameless in his sight. {...}

Romans 8

1 Therefore, there is now no condemnation for those who are in Christ Jesus,

1 Peter 2

2 Like newborn babies, crave pure spiritual milk, so that by it you may grow up in your salvation,

Ephesians 4

22 You were taught, with regard to your former way of life, to put off your old self, which is being corrupted by its deceitful desires;

Ephesians 5

15 Be very careful, then, how you live—not as unwise but as wise,

Colossians 2

6 So then, just as you received Christ Jesus as Lord, continue to live your lives in him,

1 John 2

6 Whoever claims to live in him must live as Jesus did.

1 John 1

7 But if we walk in the light, as he is in the light, we have fellowship with one another, and the blood of Jesus, his Son, purifies us from all sin. 8 If we claim to be without sin, we deceive ourselves and the truth is not in us. 9 If we confess our sins, he is faithful and just and will forgive us our sins and purify us from all unrighteousness.

Made in the USA
Monee, IL
28 July 2024

62720329R00066